Out of the Mouth of Babes

Weekly Doses of Humor and Wisdom from
My Child's Mouth to Your Heart

*Aunt Cheryl,
Thanks for always
loving & supporting me.*

K. L. WHITE-HARTMAN

Quotes Taken from A. J. W.

ISBN 978-1-0980-3113-8 (paperback)
ISBN 978-1-0980-3114-5 (digital)

Christian Faith Publishing, Inc.
832 Park Avenue
Meadville, PA 16335
www.christianfaithpublishing.com

Printed in the United States of America

To Aden,
For always giving me something to write about,
and to the Lord Most High,
who always gives me the words to write.
May all the glory and honor go to Him.

Kids often have a knack for saying the funniest (and most honest) of things, and usually at the most inconvenient of times. My child is no exception to this rule. Although we as parents are often shocked and embarrassed by the things our children say, we find humor in their words, if not in the moment, at least later on in the day. My son seems to have a gift in this department, more so than most. In fact, his sayings and doings have become so well known and cherished by my friend group that they have come to be called Adenisms. I've heard over and over again through the years that I needed to write down all the funny things he says into a book, so after all this time, here it is—your comprehensive guide to life. All from the mouth of a child. I pray this book blesses you and brings you little moments of joy. Use this as a weekly guide to refresh your spirit and reset your mind throughout the year.

From my child to your heart,
K. L. White-Hartman

Dear Reader,

The intent of this book is to give your spiritual walk a little weekly kick-start. There are verses included and application questions that you can use to think about and help you take action throughout the week. I want to speak plainly though, and let you know that reading your Bible and going through the motions of doing what's right do not make you a Christian or bring salvation. The true foundation for salvation and abundant life is a relationship with Jesus, founded on the knowledge that He died to take the punishment for our sin once and for all, and He rose again on the third day to conquer sin and death and make it possible for us to live eternally with Him in heaven. The only action required on our part to receive His free gift of salvation is to believe, first, that Jesus is God; and second, that He paid the penalty for our sin. The lessons written in this book are weekly study guides to help you grow and live the abundant life Jesus promised us we could have here on this earth if we choose to walk in His way. If you have never taken the step of accepting Jesus as your Savior, there is a verse and a simple prayer laid out below. I pray that your spiritual journey is enhanced by the messages in these pages and that you will be blessed as you progress towards all that God has called you to be.

> He then brought them out and asked, "Sirs, what must I do to be saved?" They replied, "Believe in the Lord Jesus, and you will be saved." (Acts 16:30–31a)

Lord Jesus,

I know that I am not perfect and that you are. I also know that you came to earth and died to take away the punishment for my sin. I believe you are Lord, and I accept the gift of your salvation. Thank you for allowing me to have a relationship with you. Teach me to walk in your peace and joy.

Amen.

Sharing Is Hard

When Aden was two years old, I began a very bad habit of purchasing pets as bribes to potty train him. Yup, you read that right. He earned a hermit crab, an albino frog, a whole mess of fish, some snails, and a newt. It was only after I started this trend that I found candy works just as effectively and does not require you to feed and care for a zoo; some of which creatures we still have six years later. Rookie parenting decisions aside, one day, we were at the store; and Aden found a shark statue, one of those little fish tank decorations that you put in to enhance the scenery and make your aquarium look more inviting. We took the statue home, and I proceeded to plop it into the fish tank. A little while later, Aden came wandering by and after inspecting his fish tank, asked me why *his* toy was in the fish tank. Apparently, there was some confusion as to who this was for when we picked it out at the store. In my sweetest mommy fashion, I tried to explain to his two-year-old self that this was the fishies' toy, so we must leave it in the tank. At which point, he looked at me, threw his hands in the air, and screamed, "*Them don't have hands!*"

Ah, the mind of a child is a quick-witted thing. It would only make sense that the fish could not possibly have this toy because they did not have hands to play with it. And although this story still brings me a chuckle whenever I think about it, it also reminds me that we as adults often try to reason out things in this manner too. We feel the call of God in our lives to do something kind for someone else or to reach out, and we begin to negotiate with God all the reasons why that person does not need our help or why we cannot do what we have been asked to do. But the heart of God is so much bigger, and He sees deeper than we could ever imagine. He knows the needs of each of His children, and He will often use us to meet those needs if we are willing. If you are feeling a still, small tug on your heart today to do a kind deed, do not try to reason it away. Instead, take that step of faith, and you will find you are blessed for it.

For Deeper Study

> Do not be deceived: God cannot be mocked. A man reaps what he sows. The one who sows to please his sinful nature, from that nature will reap destruction; the one who sows to please the Spirit, from the Spirit will reap eternal life. Let us not become weary in doing good, for at the proper time we will reap a harvest if we do not give up. Therefore, as we have opportunity, let us do good to all people, especially to those who belong to the family of believers. (Gal. 6:7–10)

Application Questions

Who do you need to reach out to this week? What is God calling you to do for this person?

A Completely True Tale

Have you ever had a child tell you a completely false story—one that was so unbelievable you knew immediately it was fabricated, but in the mind of the child, this story was airtight, foolproof, and completely logical? Aden has told me many of these throughout the years, but one of his best was a story he told at two years old. He came home from preschool, and sitting around the dinner table, I asked him how his day had gone. He then informed me that he has a friend named Cinnamon at school (lie clue number 1). Although the baby-naming trend has branched into some interesting names, I have yet to meet a child named Cinnamon. Aden continued describing his afternoon by letting me know that he had punched Cinnamon in the face that day. Since I had received no such report from his teacher, I was sure the validity of this story was in question.

As adults, we can easily see that Aden's silly little story about his day was false; but to him, his words seemed rational and believable. What we often forget though is that we have a tendency as grownups to lie to ourselves about our day. We tell ourselves that we weren't as productive as we could have been because our coworkers did not help us, when really, we didn't go to bed on time, and our own poor choices caused us to be poor workers. We lie to ourselves that it's okay to be rude to the people at the grocery store because we will probably never see them again. All these little lies and excuses we tell ourselves make sense in our head, but our heart knows the truth. If we are to be truly successful adults, we must stop making excuses and lies for ourselves, take responsibility for our day, and begin taking action to get where we need to be. No more inventing stories about Cinnamon. We must speak the truth to ourselves.

For Deeper Study

> Then you will know the truth, and the truth will set you free. (John 8:32)

> If we claim to be without sin, we deceive ourselves and the truth is not in us. If we confess our sins, he is faithful and just and will forgive us our sins and purify us from all unrighteousness. (1 John 1:8–9)

Application Questions

What truths do you need to own up to today? How can you start being more honest with yourself about your actions?

I Don't Need You

Have you ever gotten sick and tired of the people around you and just thought that you would rather do things on your own than continue to put up with them? I faced a similar situation with my toddler one December. One snowy day when Aden was small, I set aside my work to ask him if he would like me to play a game with him. I got out Don't Spill the Beans and set it on the table, ready to spend some quality time with my little man. Aden, however, had other plans. He promptly let me know that he wished to play by himself. He did not want me to participate. I was a little offended at the thought that my two-and-a-half-year-old would rather play a game alone than with his mommy dearest. After all, what fun was that?

Isn't it interesting though that we often do the same things as adults? We think we are better off on our own, and having help or participation from others who may not do things like we do is a waste of our time. Oh, how blind we are. We need to open our eyes and realize that each of us was created with a purpose, and no matter how different, we all can benefit from working with one another and alongside each other in the church. We must not let our pride or independence stop others from being involved in the ministry. Together, we make up the body of Christ, and it was not designed to function in pieces but rather as a whole. Become a team player today, and see how much more God can and will accomplish through your unity.

For Deeper Study

> The body is a unit, though it is made up of many parts; and though all its parts are many, they form one body. So it is with Christ. (1 Cor. 12:12)

> But in fact God has arranged the parts in the body, every one of them, just as he wanted them to be. If they were all one part, where would the body be? As it is, there are many parts, but one body. The eye cannot say to the hand, "I don't need you!" And the head cannot say to the feet, "I don't need you!" On the contrary, those parts of the body that seem to be weaker are indispensable, and the parts that we think are less honorable we treat with special honor. And the parts that are unpresentable are treated with special modesty, while our presentable parts need no special treatment. But God has combined the members of the body and has given greater honor to the parts that lacked it, so that there should be no division in the body, but that its parts should have equal concern for each other. (1 Cor. 12:18–25)

Application Questions

Who are you struggling to work with? What strengths does this person have that you don't? How can you begin to work with them in a more productive way?

I'm Having a Party Tomorrow

If you've ever had a child who is a planner, you know that they often come up with some very inventive ideas, and that often these plans do not jive with what we as parents actually have planned for the day. Aden had one of these ideas around Christmas time one year. He marched out of his room in the morning and told me that he was having a party tomorrow. He then began to list off all the people he had on his guest list: a few cousins, uncles, aunts, and of course, his Meme. I then asked him why he was not having his party today. At which point, he informed me that he was going to K-Mart today to see Santa. I'm not sure that Santa was at K-Mart, and I certainly hadn't offered to drive him there, but he was determined that those were his plans.

It's amazing that a child with no ability to drive and no ownership of anything could be so sure of what he was going to do the next two days. We are not unlike this though when we make our plans day after day and never consult the God who created us and gives us our very breath. We act as though we are in control of everything, when in reality, we should be asking God what He has planned for our days. Today, let us not be like irrational children who make plans based on our own foolish whims, but rather let us consult the One who orders our days that we might walk with purpose and achieve all we were meant to do.

For Deeper Study

> Now listen, you who say, "Today or tomorrow we will go to this or that city, spend a year there, carry on business and make money." Why you do not even know what will happen tomorrow. What is your life? You are a mist that appears for a little while and then vanishes. Instead, you ought to say, "If it is the Lord's will, we will live and do this or that." (James 4:13–15)

> In his heart a man plans his course, but the Lord determines his steps. (Prov. 16:9)

> Many are the plans in a man's heart, but it is the Lord's purpose that prevails. (Prov. 19:21)

Application Questions

What are your plans today? Have you asked God what His plans for your day are? Get in the habit of asking God to direct your plans each day.

If You, Then I'll

Have you ever had someone negotiate with you for something you wanted them to do? Growing up in a house with three brothers, this was something I did often. "If you help with my chores, then I'll play football with you." Sound familiar? Aden used one of these statements on me back when he was still small, cute, and cuddly. It was a cold January day, and I asked him if he would like to snuggle with me. His response? "You get me a drink. Then I snuggle with you." Ouch. Nothing like withholding affection until the demands have been met. Most of us would not like to be in an adult relationship where this was the case. In fact, in an adult relationship, withholding affection until demands are met might be considered abusive or quid pro quo. Yet many of us have a false view of our God operating something like this.

Have you ever thought that God would not love you, help you, or bless you until you got something right or did something for Him? Deep down, we know that God loves us without pretenses; but oftentimes, we still make conditions upon ourselves. We feel that if we messed up today, we do not deserve to ask God for something; or if we didn't go to church last week, we will not be blessed in our job this week. This mindset couldn't be farther from the truth. God is a God of unconditional love, and He is for you, no matter how far you are from Him. He loves us even in the midst of our mess, and He is there to walk with us on our journey. Next time you begin to put limits on God's love in your mind, remember that He does not require anything of you except to accept His free gift of love. Enjoy your blessings today, and live without condemnation or pressure to live perfectly. You are loved immeasurably, not because of your actions, but because of Christ's gift.

For Deeper Study

You see, at just the right time, when we were still powerless, Christ died for the ungodly. Very rarely will anyone die for a righteous man, though for a good man someone might possibly dare to die. But God demonstrates His own love for us in that while we were still sinners, Christ died for us. Since we have now been justified by his blood, how much more shall we be saved from God's wrath through Him! For if, when we were God's enemies we were reconciled to him through the death of His Son, how much more having been reconciled, shall we be saved through his life! Not only is this so, but we also rejoice in God through our Lord Jesus Christ, through whom we have now received reconciliation. (Rom. 5:6–11)

For God so loved the world that he gave his one and only Son, that whoever believes in him shall not perish but have eternal life. For God did not send his Son into the world to condemn the world, but to save the world through him. (John 3:16–17)

Application Questions

Have you been putting conditions on God's love? How can you begin to view God's love free from ties to your own actions?

Getting in Shape

I f you've ever used an at-home workout video, you may have heard the name Jillian Michaels. She is a personal trainer/fitness guru, and her workout DVDs have the power to seriously kick your butt into shape. I went through a time of using her workouts when Aden was three years old, and as a result, Aden became hooked on her videos also. He would turn the TV on each day and grab his little one-pound weights; then he would stand in front of the TV waving his arms and shouting out, "Press, press, press," in time with the movie. And if you think it is funny to watch a child attempt to work out, just imagine what we as adults look like desperately trying to imitate the fabulously fit trainers on the TV. It seems we will often do anything just to have the bodies of the people we see and perceive as fit and good looking, but are we putting as much effort into imitating God as we are into following after our earthly role models?

If we're honest with ourselves, I think we often give way too much credit to people, and we think those who we perceive as successful somehow magically have it all together. We envy them and try to emulate them, and we wonder why we can't be like those so-called stars that we put up on pedestals. The reality is, though, that as Christians, the only One we need to focus on imitating is Jesus Christ; and although there may be some great mentors out there, we have to ultimately keep our eyes focused on the One who has all life's answers. Our supreme goal should be to reflect Jesus, not any one person. Today, as you go about your day, remember to keep your eyes focused on the One who matters most. Seek to imitate Him, and you will find your life much more rewarding when you do.

For Deeper Study

Be imitators of God, therefore, as dearly loved children and live a life of love, just as Christ loved us and gave himself up for us as a fragrant offering and sacrifice to God. (Eph. 5:1–2)

You were taught, with regard to your former way of life, to put off your old self, which is being corrupted by its deceitful desires, to be made new in the attitude of your minds; and to put on the new self, created to be like God in true righteousness and holiness. (Eph. 4:22–24)

Do not conform any longer to the pattern of this world, but be transformed by the renewing of your mind. Then you will be able to test and approve what God's will is—his good and perfect will. (Rom. 12:2)

Application Questions

Who have you been looking up to lately? How can you become more like Christ in your daily life?

Table Manners

If you have ever been to a restaurant with a child, you know that eating out with small children is a dangerous game. Will they behave? Will they be quiet? Will they keep their food on their plate? Despite knowing the risks, I attempted to take Aden out one night for dinner when he was three years old. Things seemed to be going smoothly, and we were enjoying our food, when the manager approached our table and asked, "How is everything tonight?"

I turned to him to politely respond that everything was wonderful, when Aden stood up on his booth, turned to the manager, and screamed, "*Get away from me!*" I was highly embarrassed, and before I could apologize, the manager took the hint and hustled away from our table.

Although we as adults would certainly (I would hope) never be this aggressive to a person just trying to check in on us, we should be this aggressive when it comes to our thought life. Many of us do not guard our thoughts the way we should, and we often forfeit the power Christ has given us by allowing our minds to wander wherever they please. We need to get very good at not only recognizing, but also repelling negative, unwholesome, and false thinking. Maybe, like Aden, we need to tell a thought, "*Get away from me!*" You were given power and authority from Christ. Begin using it today to cast down thoughts that are not from God. Your mind is a valuable gift. Make sure you protect it.

For Deeper Study

> We demolish arguments and every pretension that sets itself up against the knowledge of God, and we take captive every thought to make it obedient to Christ. (2 Cor. 10:5)

> Finally, brothers, whatever is true, whatever is noble, whatever is right, whatever is pure, whatever is lovely, whatever is admirable—if anything is excellent or praiseworthy—think about such things. (Phil. 4:8)

Application Questions

What wrong thinking have you been allowing in your life? What steps can you take to change your thinking today?

All Grown Up

A den and I often have some of our most interesting conversations while driving in the car. Perhaps it is because he has more time to think when he cannot run around, and he has me as a captive audience since I cannot leave the area. Some of his best quotes have happened while we were traveling down the road. One February, we were driving in the car when Aden said from the back seat, "I'm a big people."

Slightly confused by his wording, I asked, "You are?"

He then explained, "Yes, I'm a big kid, and big kids are big persons, so I'm a big people."

Seems logical I guess. Although I think we had different opinions on what being big means. Aden was probably not more than three years old at this time and stood only about two-and-a-half feet tall, but to him, he was a "big people."

Similarly, when we evaluate ourselves, we often tend to have exaggerated versions of ourselves and our spirituality, but sometimes we need to look at what God says makes us mature. God says our maturity stems from an understanding of His truths. Are you growing and developing in your knowledge of God and His word? If not, maybe you need to evaluate where you actually are in your spiritual growth. Maybe it's time for you to put more dedicated time and effort into learning and absorbing God's truths so you can become the person He has called you to be. Don't stay stuck as a spiritual child, only thinking you are "big," but in reality, still only knowing the basics. Make time with God a priority and begin to grow in Him today.

For Deeper Study

> If fact, though by this time you ought to be teachers, you need someone to teach you the elementary truths of God's work all over again. You need milk, not solid food! Anyone who lives on milk, being still an infant, is not acquainted with the teaching about righteousness. But solid food is for the mature, who by constant use have trained themselves to distinguish good from evil. (Heb. 5:12–14)

> Therefore let us leave the elementary teachings about Christ and go on to maturity. (Heb. 6:1a)

Application Questions

How can you begin to grow and become more spiritually mature? What steps do you need to take today?

What I Have to Offer

S ometimes when we give children directions, we have one idea in mind, and they have another. One such incident happened when I asked Aden to go get me a towel out of the bathroom. There had been a spill (this happens often when you have a small child and several dogs), and I needed him to go get a towel so I could begin drying up the mess. Aden went straight into the bathroom, but he did not return immediately, and he seemed to be taking an inordinately long time to do the simple task of grabbing a towel. He did finally return though, but not with the towel I had asked him to bring. He carefully opened his hands to display to me a handful of shredded toilet paper, which he had meticulously pulled off the roll. Holding it out to me, he said apologetically, "This is all I could get." How precious and heartfelt his effort was, despite not being what I needed for the task.

Although I could not work with the small gift Aden was giving me, God can work with the small gifts we hold out to Him. God has the amazing ability to multiply our efforts when we give them to Him. We might not view what we have as much, but God can use whatever we have to do great things. Like the widow in the book of 1 Kings, God can take our meager supply and, combined with His infinite stores, miraculous blessings can occur. Whatever you have today, do not withhold it from doing God's will. Live with an open hand and heart to God's calling, and you will find the blessings of the Lord will cause your cup to overflow.

For Deeper Study

Then the word of the Lord came to him: [Elijah] "Go at once to Zarephath of Sidon and stay there. I have commanded a widow in the place to supply you with food." So he went to Zarephath. When he came to the town gate, a widow was there gathering sticks. He called to her and asked, "Would you bring me a little water in a jar so I may have a drink?" As she was going to get it, he called, "And bring me, please, a piece of bread." "As surely as the Lord your God lives," she replied, "I don't have any bread—only a handful of flour in a jar and a little oil in a jug. I am gathering a few sticks to take home and make a meal for myself and my son, that we may eat it—and die." Elijah said to her, "Don't be afraid. Go home and do as you have said. But first make a small cake of bread for me from what you have and bring it to me, and then make something for yourself and your son. For this is what the Lord, the God of Israel, says: 'The jar of flour will not be used up and the jug of oil will not run dry until the day the Lord gives rain on the land.'" She went away and did as Elijah had told her. So there was food every day for Elijah and for the woman and her family. For the jar of flour was not used up and the jug of oil did not run dry, in keeping with the word of the Lord spoken by Elijah. (1 Kings 17:8–16)

Application Question

What can you give to God this week from your time, talents, or resources?

I Don't Know You

My son Aden has oppositional defiant disorder, so he started from a very young age with trying to act out when we were around other people and doing things which he thought would be purposefully hurtful or embarrassing in public. At the age of almost four, each trip to the grocery store was a full-on battle of wills and usually resulted in tears for all parties involved. On one such day, when Aden was being particularly bad, he threw himself on the floor at the checkout and refused to move. I bent over, grabbed him by the arm, and began my best mommy threat, "Aden, if you don't get up now…"

But before I could finish my sentence, he looked around at all the curious onlookers; and in his most pitiful voice yelled out, "I don't know you!" I was mortified. It's a good thing he looks so much like me, or I may not have made it out of the store without being arrested. I often joke since then that I couldn't deny him if I tried.

I wonder, though, how often we as Christians deny our Savior by our words and actions. Do people know we belong to Christ by the way we act? Or is there some doubt as to whose child we really are? It's time we take a look at the "fruit" in our lives and ask ourselves truthfully whom our behavior is representing. If your life leaves your status in question, maybe it is time to start asking yourself the old question, "What would Jesus do?" Our actions should reflect our Savior, who made it his goal to reflect the Father. Start walking the walk today and be an example of Christ's love so all who meet you know Who you belong to.

For Deeper Study

Thus by their fruit you will recognize them. (Matt. 7:20)

Before long, the world will not see me anymore, but you will see me. Because I live, you also will live. On that day you will realize that I am in my Father, and you are in me, and I am in you. Whoever has my commands and obeys them, he is the one who loves me. He who loves me will be loved by my Father, and I too will love him and show myself to him. (John 14:19–21)

Yet to all who received him, to those who believed in his name, he gave the right to become children of God. (John 1:12)

Application Questions

Do your actions demonstrate who you belong to? How can you begin to display more "fruit" in your life?

I Can Do This

Sometimes, we as adults take for granted how easily we can do simple tasks that children have not yet mastered. Pouring juice, tying shoes, and buttoning pants are just a few of the small things in life which seem baffling to children yet so insignificant to us. One day, at three years old, Aden decided he wanted to help me fold and put away laundry. Knowing that he probably would not be much actual help, but appreciating his desire to try, I handed him a shirt and asked him to put it on the hanger. I continued folding and putting away laundry, and when I came back in a few minutes, he was still wrestling the shirt. I stood back and kept folding, waiting to see what would happen. Aden determinedly kept working, saying out loud to himself, "I'm a big boy. I can do this!" His self-confidence and perseverance in the face of this obstacle were adorable, but also inspiring.

Oftentimes, we as adults forget in the face of seemingly insurmountable tasks that our God is big, and we are given the ability to do *all* things through Christ. Nothing is impossible for God, and it's time we start speaking that truth rather than confessing our doubt and defeat. If you are facing a difficult situation today, begin to speak words of victory and strength. Do not tear yourself down by your words, but instead, empower yourself with God's Word. You can do this! You have a big God!

For Deeper Study

> Jesus looked at them and said, "With man this is impossible, but with God all things are possible." (Matt. 19:26)

> I can do everything through Him who gives me strength. (Phil. 4:13)

> I tell you the truth, if you have faith as small as a mustard seed, you can say to this mountain, "Move from here to there" and it will move. Nothing will be impossible for you. (Matt. 17:20b)

Application Questions

Where in your life have you been doubting your ability to succeed? How can you begin to exercise your faith in this area?

Vengeance Is Mine

Kids often say exactly what they are thinking, even if that thought is not really something that should be said out loud. Aden, like many "only children," tends to be a little selfish when it comes to other kids, and he is very swift to administer justice when he feels he has been wronged. Case in point, one day while playing with his cousin, who is much smaller than him, he was playing a little rough. I warned him, "Please be careful that you don't smash Emma."

Aden very directly retorted to me, "She needs smashed."

Now what she had possibly done to deserve a smashing, I wasn't sure; but Aden had no remorse or pity for her as he felt if he did hurt her, she would be getting what she deserved.

Oh, how like this we are when we take matters into our own hands, or wish that a person who wronged us would receive some type of punishment. We have a desire to right the perceived wrong, and oftentimes, we are willing to take matters into our own hands with an unkind word or deed. We need to remember, though, that as Christ's ambassadors, it is our job not to repay evil, but to demonstrate love and grace instead. We need to practice the forgiveness and mercy Christ has shown us and extend a loving hand to those who hurt us. God is the one who will right the wrongs. It is up to us to forgive and move on, and when we follow God's instructions in this, we can be sure we will reap a blessing in our lives.

For Deeper Study

> Finally, all of you, live in harmony with one another; be sympathetic, love as brothers, be compassionate and humble. Do not repay evil with evil or insult with insult, but with blessing, because to this you were called so that you may inherit a blessing. (1 Pet. 3:8–9)

> But I tell you, love your enemies and pray for those who persecute you. (Matt. 5:44)

Application Questions

Have you been holding on to a wrong someone has done? Begin today to let go of the injustices against you and let God handle the rest.

The Little Things

If you have ever been woken up in the middle of the night, you know that it is extremely irritating, especially if you are woken for an insignificant reason. Aden has always been a poor sleeper, so from the time he was born, I have become accustomed to being awakened at all hours of the night. One particular night though, Aden came into my bedroom at 4:30 a.m., sobbing at the top of his lungs. I jumped up and asked him what was wrong. Had he fallen out of bed? Did he have a bad dream? Aden held up his hands in front of his face at arm's length and cried out, "I don't like my fingers!" Oh, the silly things our minds come up with when we are not quite awake. I had a good laugh over this one and convinced him to get back into his bed.

How often our silly requests and minuscule complaints must seem to God like the child who complains about his fingers in the night, yet God, in his graciousness and compassion, does not turn us away. He does not laugh at us or tell us it's not important. He gives us the command instead to "cast our cares." He is willing to take every worry and concern we have because we matter to Him. Know today that you are so valuable to God. He loves you and cares about whatever is bothering you, and He is willing to take your burden, no matter how small or how large. Give God your cares today and begin to live with a new freedom and peace.

For Deeper Study

> Cast all your anxiety on him because He cares for you. (1 Pet. 5:7)

> Look at the birds of the air; they do not sow or reap or store away in barns, and yet your heavenly Father feeds them. Are you not much more valuable than they? Who of you by worrying can add a single hour to his life? (Matt. 6:26–27)

Application Question

What cares have you been holding on to? Take them to God in prayer and release them for Him to carry.

Running Away

Sometimes as children, we get the misguided idea that running away from home might be a good solution to our problems. As small children, we may threaten but never follow through; and as teenagers, maybe some of us actually tried. But for most of us, we found out that home is much better than being alone out in the world. Aden has never tried to run away, but he did consider it briefly around four years old. I had reprimanded him for being wild and punching things, and as he saw nothing wrong with this behavior, he was rather unhappy with me. After a minute of thinking, he turned to me and asked angrily, "Why can't you just let me run away? Then, I can punch whatever I want!"

Isn't it true though that we often take this same attitude with God? We try to run away in hopes that we can distance ourselves from Him and not have to follow through with obedience. When we are struggling with sin, we try to put up a wall between ourselves and God, yet it is during these very times that we need God the most. We have to remember that God loves us no matter what, and He wants to redeem us and forgive us from our sinful nature. Stop running *from* God, and start running *to* Him instead. Like the prodigal son, choose to return home and find that you were loved and forgiven all along. Life in His presence is far better than living alone out in the world.

For Deeper Study

Therefore, there is now no condemnation for those who are in Christ Jesus, because through Christ Jesus the law of the Spirit of life set me free from the law of sin and death. (Rom. 8:1–2)

The Lord is not slow in keeping his promise, as some understand slowness. He is patient with you, not wanting anyone to perish, but everyone to come to repentance. (2 Pet. 3:9)

But while he was still a long way off, his father saw him and was filled with compassion for him; he ran to his son, threw his arms around him and kissed him. (Luke 15:20b)

Application Question

Have you been struggling with an area of sin and trying to run from God? Seek God about your sin, and allow Him to work in your life and help you overcome and obey.

How Tall Are You?

It seems that small children have a fascination with trying to grow up and being as big as their mommies and daddies. Aden was three years old when he climbed up on a chair one day and asked, "Mom, am I pie as you?"

I responded a bit quizzically, "You mean *high*? Like are you as tall as me?"

Aden repeated, "Yes, am I pie as you?"

Laughing a bit at his inability to grasp the slight word difference, I answered, "You're not quite as high as me yet, buddy." Adding, "It's *high*, not *pie*."

Aden is persistent though, and he insisted, "I think I'm as pie as you."

Giving a sigh of defeat, I said, "Okay, yup. You are as pie as me."

How funny the thoughts that children get and the ways that they express them, but how like them we are when we go to God with our ideas. We are much like the small child, straining to get God to see things our way, thinking we know best. When in reality, He has a much higher perspective, and He tells us that His thoughts and ways far exceed anything we could come up with on our own. We simply need to trust Him rather than our own small perceptions of things. If you are feeling a bit wise in your own mind this week, take some time to really ask God what His perspective on things is and how He wants you to proceed. You may just find that He has a much better plan than anything you could have conceived of alone. After all, we are not as "pie" as Him.

For Deeper Study

"For my thoughts are not your thoughts, neither are your ways my ways," declares the Lord. "As the heavens are higher than the earth, so are my ways higher than your ways and my thoughts than your thoughts." (Isa. 55:8–9)

Trust in the Lord with all your heart and lean not on your own understanding; in all your ways acknowledge Him and He will make your paths straight. (Prov. 3:5–6)

Application Questions

What areas of your life have you been leaning on your own understanding in? Is there something you need to ask for God's opinion about?

How Do I Look?

Children often have misconceptions of some of the routines we as adults have. They don't understand some of the seemingly simple things we do, so their attempts to mimic us are very comical. I have a penchant for perfume, and consequentially, Aden has often seen me trying bottles of perfume at stores whenever we go out and about shopping. Naturally then, when he went to the store with his aunt one day, he felt the need to do the same. Seeing a sample bottle of perfume, he grabbed it from the shelf, sprayed it dutifully upon his face, and turning to his aunt asked, "Does my face look pretty?" Clearly, he has missed the idea. Perfume is not for spraying on the face, nor does it enhance your appearance; but to a child's mind, this seemed like the right course of action. And of course, the way to verify that it had been applied correctly was to check with someone else for their approval.

Isn't this so like us? We do what we can to look good, picking out clothes, jewelry, cologne, and makeup, all to win the approval of others and make sure we look the part of the person we are trying to portray. But I wonder if we invest as much time on perfecting our inner person as we do our outer appearance. The Bible tells us that it's not what we put on our body that matters, but rather what we put in it from a spiritual standpoint. We need to be investing our time and energy into developing our characters and hearts to reflect the character and heart of God. Only then will we find that we truly radiate with beauty from the inside out. Today, as you prepare yourself to go to work, meet with friends, or simply get on with your day, take time to groom your inner person as well. You will find that what's inside is much more important to our life than what others see as our outer being. Good looks may initially attract people to you, but if you do not have a good attitude and good things flowing from your Spirit, you will very quickly find yourself pushing people away.

If you want to make a lasting impact on others and develop deeper relationships, the secret is not found in what you wear, but in what you have stored up inside you.

For Deeper Study

> Your beauty should not come from outward adornment, such as braided hair and the wearing of gold jewelry and fine clothes. Instead, it should be that of your inner self, and the unfading beauty of a gentle and quiet spirit, which is of great worth in God's sight. (1 Pet. 3:3–4)

> The good man brings good things out of the good stored up in his heart, and the evil man brings evil things out of the evil stored up in his heart. For out of the overflow of his heart his mouth speaks. (Luke 6:45)

Application Questions

What things are you bringing forth in your life? How can you work on changing what you're producing?

I'll Show You

Aden has a rather boisterous personality, and he is never afraid to express himself, especially when he feels an injustice has been done against him. We have had many conversations over the years about how to respond when others do things we don't like. One day, just before his fourth birthday, Aden had a few friends at the house; and I was visiting with their mothers. All was going well until I began to hear screaming from the backyard. I quickly dismissed myself from the conversation and started heading that way to investigate, knowing that my child was probably at the center of the incident. Before I made it very far though, Aden came striding confidently around the corner of the house as if he already knew I would be seeking the source of the disturbance. He walked up to me very assuredly and said, "Ya, he's crying because he took my toy, so I punched him in the face," as if this was a perfectly logical explanation. Obviously, this was the correct way to deal with the situation, and parental involvement was not needed here. Aden, of course, received a speedy correction and learned that punching someone was not an acceptable way to respond to having a toy taken.

As adults, we need to be cautious that we do not fall into a mindset of justifying mistreatment of others based on their treatment of us. We are called to love and pray for those who are our "enemies," which means that even if we don't like their behavior, we are not to respond with negative retaliation. This might mean that you need to bite your tongue when that person cuts you in line at the grocery store, or you may need to pray for the coworker who gossips about you rather than starting gossip about her. Maybe your husband or wife did something to tick you off this morning, and you feel the need to get even. Stop and think about what kind of reputation your actions are creating for you. Do people see you as someone who follows God and quickly forgives, or do they know that you will be quick to seek your own justice? Check your responses today and begin retaliating with good rather than evil. Let God be the judge of the situation. We are simply called to love.

For Deeper Study

> But I tell you who hear me: Love your enemies, do good to those who hate you, bless those who curse you, pray for those who mistreat you. If someone strikes you on one cheek, turn to him the other also. If someone takes your cloak, do not stop him from taking your tunic. Give to everyone who asks you, and if anyone takes what belongs to you, do not demand it back. Do to others as you would have them do to you. If you love those who love you, what credit is that to you? Even "sinners" love those who love them. And if you do good to those who are good to you, what credit is that to you? Even "sinners" do that. And if you lend to those from whom you expect repayment, what credit is that to you? Even "sinners" lend to "sinners," expecting to be repaid in full. But love your enemies, do good to them, and lend to them without expecting to get anything back. Then your reward will be great, and you will be sons of the Most High, because He is kind to the ungrateful and wicked. Be merciful, just as your Father is merciful. (Luke 6:27–36)

Application Questions

Who do you need to forgive today? Have you been taking matters into your own hands? How can you begin to view those who hurt you with the love of Christ?

An Unwelcome Interruption

If you spend any amount of time around me, you will very quickly learn that I have a great love for dogs. We have several, and I have a tendency to add a new puppy every three years or so. As such, we spend a lot of time cleaning up after our dogs and dealing with the necessary evils of house training. It was no surprise to me then when a few days after getting our latest puppy, Aden came to me and announced, "There is puppy pee on the floor."

I sighed and said, "Okay," and returned to what I was doing. I figured there was no harm in leaving it there a minute longer while I finished my task.

Aden, however, had other ideas. He sighed exasperatedly and said, "Um, I left all my work I had to do just so I could look around for pee, so what do you say?" I laughed at this one. What work could a five-year-old possibly have to do that was so important? I thanked him for his time, adding that I was sorry he had to interrupt his busy schedule.

Don't we do this same thing to God, though? We see an act of charity we should do, or we take time out of our week to pray for someone, and we expect God to give us a big applause, as if our efforts are so great, and it is such a big deal to take time out of what we have planned to help others. We forget, though, that every minute we have is from God, and we should be honored to get to spend time doing something for Him, not the other way around. You may have a very busy life, and there's nothing wrong with that, but make sure that you put the most important things first. Your relationship with God and any task He asks you to do should always come before your own agenda. Don't get sidetracked with all the things you "have" to do. The only thing we really "need" to do is what God has called us to do. Give Him your time today, and you will find He can accomplish far more with your day than you could have.

For Deeper Study

As Jesus and his disciples were on their way, He came to a village where a woman named Martha opened her home to him. She had a sister called Mary, who sat at the Lord's feet listening to what He said. But Martha was distracted by all the preparations that had to be made. She came to Him and asked, "Lord, don't you care that my sister has left me to do the work by myself? Tell her to help me!"

"Martha, Martha," the Lord answered, "you are worried and upset about many things, but only one thing is needed. Mary has chosen what is better, and it will not be taken away from her." (Luke 10:38–42)

Application Question

How can you begin to serve God with your time this week?

The "More" Epidemic

A den and I have always loved going out to eat together, so it is something we do frequently. One of Aden's favorite "fast food" restaurants is Subway. He always gets a pepperoni sub with black olives and bacon. And from the time he was a little boy, I had to start ordering him a full twelve-inch sub. One day, before I started this practice, we had ordered our subs, chips, and drinks. I got myself a twelve-inch sub and Aden a six-inch. I figured that was sufficient for a five-year-old child. We sat down to eat, unwrapped our subs, and Aden looked from his sub to my sub. He very quickly realized the difference, and without missing a beat, he asked, "Where's the other half of mine?"

As a parent, it's frustrating to have my child fail to appreciate the things I get for him and always demand more; but oftentimes, we treat God in the same manner. We spend so much time complaining about what we don't have that we forget to look at all the amazing blessings that God has given us. Today, make a point to look around you and be thankful for what you see. You can live with gratitude and contentment rather than with grumbling and demanding. Thankfulness will change your perspective and help you live more peacefully and joyfully, no matter what circumstance you find yourself in. Find some things to appreciate today, and don't let complaints crowd out the good things in your life.

For Deeper Study

> Do everything without complaining or arguing. (Phil. 2:14)

> This is the day the Lord has made; let us rejoice and be glad in it. (Ps. 118:24)

> I have learned to be content whatever the circumstances. (Phil. 4:11b)

Application Questions

Where can you learn to be more content in your life? What things are you thankful for this week?

Self-Sabotage

M ost of us enjoy doing things when they are going our way, and we get frustrated and don't want to do things when they do not go our way. This is characteristic of human nature. We have inside us a desire to succeed, and we do not want to do things which make us feel as though we are not succeeding. You can imagine my frustration then when one day, I made an attempt to build a block tower with Aden. He was two years old and more interested in destroying what I was making than helping build it. After he had knocked down my block tower for what felt like the hundredth time, he looked at me and angrily yelled, "I don't want to play this game anymore!"

To which I responded, "Me either, buddy. Me either."

You would think that because he was the one ruining the game, Aden would have realized that the way to fix the problem was to just quit knocking the blocks down, but we do the same things when we refuse to do as God has asked us to do in our lives. We stumble and fall over the same sins over and over again when we could just follow God's plan for our lives. In a sense, we are knocking over our own tower when we choose to go our own way. We often know that our poor choice is going to hurt us, but we choose to do it anyway. Whatever stubborn behavior you are holding on to today, determine that you will not allow it to sabotage your progress anymore. Make a choice to do what you know is right and watch your life bloom and grow as a result.

For Deeper Study

> But Daniel resolved not to defile himself. (Dan. 1:8a)

> If you do what is right, will you not be accepted? But if you do not do what is right, sin is crouching at your door; it desires to have you, but you must master it. (Gen. 4:7)

Application Questions

What wrong behaviors are you holding on to in your life? What action steps do you need to take to remove these behaviors? Are there good behaviors you know you need to start? How can you take a step in the right direction today?

Fighting Lions

It is always amusing to me the perceptions that children have of the world and things around them. As a three-year-old boy, Aden was riding in the car with me when he suddenly piped up, "I can use my magical powers to destroy stuff." He then quickly added, "But I can't fight lions. They are too good of fighters. They like, eat you or something. Is that true, Mom?" And while it is true that fighting a lion is probably a bad choice, and they will "like eat you or something," the Bible specifically records multiple incidences when God delivered his people from lions.

We serve a great and mighty God, and He can deliver us from any circumstance, no matter how impossible or overwhelming it seems. Let these stories about defeating lions be your reminder that God is with you today, and He can deliver you from whatever you are facing.

For Deeper Study

Samson went down to Timnah together with his father and mother. As they approached the vineyards of Timnah, suddenly a young lion came roaring toward him. The Spirit of the Lord came upon him in power so that he tore the lion apart with his bare hands as he might have torn a young goat. (Judg. 14:5–6a)

Benaiah son of Jehoiada was a valiant fighter from Kabzeel, who performed great exploits. He struck down two of Moab's best men. He also went down into a pit on a snowy day and killed a lion. (2 Sam. 23:20)

At the first light of dawn, the king got up and hurried to the lions' den. When he came near the den, he called to Daniel in an anguished voice, "Daniel, servant of the living God, has your God whom you serve continually, been able to rescue you from the lions?" Daniel answered, "O king, live forever! My God sent his angel, and he shut the mouths of the lions. They have not hurt me because I was found innocent in his sight. Nor have I ever done any wrong before you, O king." (Dan. 6:19–22)

The Lord who delivered me from the paw of the lion and the paw of the bear will deliver me from the hand of this Philistine. (1 Sam. 17:37)

Application Question

What "lions" are you up against in your life today? Meditate on God's Word and be reminded that He is more powerful than anything you face this week.

Babies and Stuff

Children often have very inquisitive minds, and because there are many things which are not yet appropriate to share with them, they may ask some very funny questions. Aden came marching into the room one day at four years old and demanded to know, "How do I grow a baby if I'm not a girl?" I laughed and told him he would have to find a girl to grow a baby for him. No way was I having *that* talk with a four-year-old.

We often ask these same silly questions of God, though. We don't know the answer to something, and rather than trust that He has a plan and will reveal it when we are ready, we go to Him demanding answers. Moses did this when he was asked by God to go to Egypt and deliver the Israelites from the hand of Pharaoh. Rather than accept that God obviously wouldn't ask him to do something that He hadn't already created a plan for, Moses began to ask every question he could think of to try to get out of going. Next time you feel God's call on your life, put aside your questions and instead trust that He knows more than you do. He will give us the answers when we need them. Until then, learn to walk by faith, and you will be blessed for it.

For Deeper Study

> But Moses said to God, "Who am I, that I should go to Pharaoh and bring the Israelites out of Egypt?" And God said, "I will be with you." (Exod. 3:11–12a)

> Moses answered, "What if they do not believe me or listen to me and say, 'The Lord did not appear to you'?" (Exod. 4:1)

> Moses said to the Lord, "O Lord, I have never been eloquent, neither in the past nor since you have spoken to your servant. I am slow of speech and tongue." The Lord said to him, "Who gave man his mouth? Who makes him deaf or mute? Who gives him sight or makes him blind? Is it not I, the Lord? Now go; I will help you speak and will teach you what to say." (Exod. 4:10–12)

Application Question

What have you been questioning God about lately? Entrust your doubts to God and have faith that He knows the answers.

Who's the Judge?

Aden has always had the ability to get himself into trouble through his behavior at school and somehow come out thinking he is the victim in the situation. This has led to many an interesting conversation over the years, but one particular day, Aden came home from kindergarten and told me indignantly, "Mom, today, someone judged me for putting up my middle finger twice." I did my best to stifle a laugh and calmly explained to him that there were some things he shouldn't do (putting up his middle finger, for example). And that if he did those things, other people might feel offended, and they might get upset about it. And although in this case, Aden was most certainly in the wrong, I think a lot of us tend to have this same mindset.

We go about our day, and we are always judging the "wrong" things that other people do, but we tend to excuse the "wrong" things that we do because we know the reasons. We don't think we are guilty for cutting off the other person in traffic because obviously, we had more important things to do than them. We have no problem explaining away why we were late to pick up our child from school today, but we certainly didn't hesitate to tell others about our coworker who had to call off work this morning. We must begin to really watch what we say and how we react to others. We have been given grace by God, and we must learn to extend this to everyone around us. We were not called to judge others, only to love them. Today, when someone offends you or makes you upset, give them the same grace you would give yourself. Try to see their actions through a different lens and realize that it's not your job to criticize or condemn them. Show love and forgiveness instead.

For Deeper Study

> Do not judge, or you too will be judged. (Matt. 7:1)

> But to each one of us grace has been given as Christ appointed it. (Eph. 4:7)

> Then Peter came to Jesus and asked, "Lord, how many times shall I forgive my brother when he sins against me? Up to seven times?" Jesus answered, "I tell you, not seven times, but seventy-seven times." (Matt. 18:21–22)

Application Questions

Is there someone you need to extend grace to today? How can you become more understanding of other people and their situations? How can you demonstrate God's grace in your interactions with other people today?

The Reason Why

If you have ever struggled with a child who pees the bed, you know how frustrating it is. Washing sheets, blankets, pillows, and stuffed animals daily, along with ruined mattresses, and the never-ending pee smell in the house are just a few of the joys of nighttime potty training. One day, in my exasperation, I asked Aden why he would not get out of bed and walk to the bathroom at night. I had left pretty much every light in the entire house on for him, and it was not a far walk. Aden responded very matter-of-factly by telling me that he could not walk to the bathroom at night because there was a snake in our house. I can assure you this was not at all the case, but in his mind, it seemed like a very valid excuse.

I wonder if God shakes his head at us in this same manner when we give Him our excuses for not doing what He calls us to do. Perhaps you've tried the "I don't have time," "I'm not qualified," or "I'm not sure how I could afford to do that" excuses with God. If you have, know that He is not derailed by our excuses. He will keep nudging us with that still, small voice to get ourselves in line with His will for our lives. If you are making excuses today, start to set them aside and trust the provision and guidance of God. After all, He will not call you to anything that He cannot equip you to do. Many great leaders in the Bible were initially terrified and made excuses when God first called them, but with a little encouragement from God, they stepped out into what they needed to do. Take a step of faith in the right direction this week and watch God open the doors for you to walk through.

For Deeper Study

> The Lord turned to him [Gideon] and said, "Go in the strength you have and save Israel out of Midian's hand. Am I not sending you?" "But Lord," Gideon asked, "how can I save Israel? My clan is the weakest in Manasseh, and I am the least in my family." The Lord answered, "I will be with you, and you will strike down all the Midianites together." (Judg. 6:14–16)

> Have I not commanded you? Be strong and courageous. Do not be terrified; do not be discouraged, for the Lord your God will be with you wherever you go. (Josh. 1:9)

> "Do not be afraid of them, for I am with you and will rescue you," declares the Lord. (Jer. 1:8)

Application Questions

Where have you been making excuses and letting fear rule in your life? What action do you need to take this week?

Persistence Pays

Have you ever been around a child that will…not…leave…you…alone? Aden is a particularly persistent kid, and he started one morning very early with, "Can we play a game, Mom? Mom? Mom? Can we play a game?" Over and over and over—before coffee.

Finally, turning to Aden, I said, "Let's play the 'leave mommy alone for five minutes till she finishes her coffee' game. It's my favorite." Although we have to admit that this kind of behavior can be extremely aggravating, we also have to admit that it is often effective. Persistent kids, and adults, who refuse to take "no" for an answer often achieve far more than those who are not willing to pursue what they want.

The Bible itself encourages us to use this same attitude when we pray. The persistence of a child in asking for something is the same persistence we should use with our God when we go before Him in prayer. He wants to grant us blessings, but we must ask Him, and keep asking Him daily. Doing so reaffirms our faith in Him and His desire to lavish us with his love. Do not give up today. Keep asking for God to open doors and shower you with favor. Your persistence will be rewarded greatly.

For Deeper Study

Then Jesus told his disciples a parable to show them that they should always pray and not give up. He said, "In a certain town there was a judge who neither feared God nor cared about men. And there was a widow in that town who kept coming to him with the plea, 'Grant me justice against my adversary.' For some time he refused. But finally he said to himself, 'Even though I don't fear God or care about men, yet because this widow keeps bothering me, I will see that she gets justice, so that she won't eventually wear me out with her coming!'" And the Lord said, "Listen to what the unjust judge says. And will not God bring about justice for His chosen ones, who cry out to Him day and night? Will He keep putting them off?" (Luke 18:1–7)

Ask and it will be given to you; seek and you will find; knock and the door will be opened to you. For everyone who asks receives; he who seeks finds; and to him who knocks, the door will be opened. (Matt. 7:7–8)

Application Questions

What have you been asking God for in prayer? How can you be more persistent with your prayers this week?

Reading a Book

Watching a child learn to read and gain an appreciation for books has something magical about it. I loved reading with Aden, and I am so glad he has picked up that love of books as well. But as a young reader, some texts are simply too hard to understand, and if you are Aden, you just continue pretending to read, making up what it says along the way. When he was five, Aden sat, busily "reading" a book about dinosaurs; and as he read, he told me, "Velociraptors can go 20,000 miles in one hour."

With my eyebrows raised in doubt, I asked him, "Really?"

"Ya," he responded. "I think that's what it says, but I can't really read this page very good." Clearly, something was lost in translation, but that did not stop him from attempting to read.

What we can be sure of, though, is this. If we take the time to invest in reading God's Word, the Bible tells us that we will not come away empty-handed. God has placed lessons and messages in His Word, and He promises that His Word will always set out to do what it was meant to do. Make it a priority to read God's Word daily, and you will begin to see the results of it throughout your life. You may not realize it at first, but little by little, the scripture will change you if you stay open to its message. Start a new reading habit today and find out just how much God can show you through His Word.

For Deeper Study

> So is my word that goes out from my mouth: It will not return to Me empty, but will accomplish what I desire and achieve the purpose for which I sent it. (Isa. 55:11)

> Blessed is the man who does not walk in the counsel of the wicked or stand in the way of sinners or sit in the seat of mockers. But his delight is in the law of the Lord, and on his law he meditates day and night. (Ps. 1:1–2)

> Your statutes are my heritage forever; they are the joy of my heart. (Ps. 119:111)

Application Questions

How often do you make time to read the Word of God? How can you increase this habit in your life?

Identity Search

We as adults often seem to struggle with who we are and what our purpose is. We've heard of the "identity crisis" or "midlife crisis," and you may have seen someone go through this. But children seem to have an innate sense of who they are. Ask a child what they want to be when they grow up, and they will always have a ready answer. Perhaps it is because they have not yet learned of limitations. They have nothing standing in their way. They can be whatever they want to be. Aden told me very boldly at five years old, "Sometimes, I'm Batman, and sometimes," pausing a moment to ponder, "I'm always Batman." Nothing like knowing exactly who you are.

Although we, in our humanness, may wrestle with self-doubt, we can have the confidence that our God does not change. He is consistent, and we can know that He will be there each and every day, the same as He has always been and will always be. We can rest in the fact that we don't have to guess about God's goodness, grace, love, or faithfulness. He is unchanging from age to age. If you are struggling with who you are or where you belong today, start with the One who has a firm foundation. Begin to find your identity in Him, and you will no longer have to waver back and forth, plagued by questions of self-doubt. You can know for sure who you are in Christ.

For Deeper Study

> Jesus is the same yesterday and today and forever.
> (Heb. 13:8)

> For in Him we live and move and have our being.
> (Acts 17:28a)

Application Question

Have you been doubting or feeling confused about your identity? Begin reading God's Word and seeing what He says about His children. Take His Words to heart and begin to claim your place as a child of the King.

What You Don't Know

Children like to think they are fooling us as parents. They enjoy thinking they are getting away with something we don't know about. Many times, we are fully aware of just what they are up to, but every once in a while, they manage to actually dupe us, and then it gets a little hairy. Aden pulled a doozy one day when he was three years old. We had been visiting some family, and at the end of the day, when I packed him into the car seat and drove away, all seemed normal. We drove home without a hint of treachery, but the moment we got inside, Aden pulled a cell phone from inside his pants and proudly announced, "Look what I've got!" I was mortified! My child had stolen a cell phone. Not only that, but he had hidden it inside his pants and had the peace of mind to keep quiet about it all the way home. I was in shock as I drove the whole way back to return it to the missing party. Of course, all our friends and family got a good laugh out of the story.

Unlike us as parents, God does not miss anything. He is not fooled. He knows exactly what we are up to. He knows our thoughts and our actions. There is nothing we can hide from Him even when we wish we could. Whatever is causing you to put up a wall or run from God today, surrender it. God already knows about it, and He is waiting to forgive you and have a relationship with you again. You do not have to try to hide. You are loved and accepted just as you are, right where you are. Run to God today and fling open the door of your heart. Let Him help you restore the broken and dirty places. He longs to make you whole.

For Deeper Study

O Lord, You have searched me and You know me. You know when I sit and when I rise; You perceive my thoughts from afar. You discern my going out and my lying down; You are familiar with all my ways. Before a word is on my tongue You know it completely, O Lord. (Ps. 139:1–4)

Where can I go from your Spirit? Where can I flee from your presence? (Ps. 139:7)

If I say, "Surely the darkness will hide me and the light become night around me," even the darkness will not be dark to you; the night will shine like the day, for darkness is as light to you. (Ps. 139:11–12)

Application Questions

What have you been trying to hide from God? How can you open your heart and surrender it to Him today?

What Friends Are For

Sometimes, a good friend and a little bit of honesty is all we need to get ourselves back on the right track. It seems that those who know us best and are not afraid to speak truth to us can help us to see where we are stumbling and help us get over any hurdles we may be facing. Aden has a good friend who often calls him out on his behavior, and as a mother, I can really appreciate him having a peer to validate what I'm saying. One such incident occurred when Aden was six, and he had this friend over. Aden was whining and complaining about something, and I said to him sternly, "Are you whining? You need to stop."

The whining continued, however, until his friend piped up, "Man up!" He yelled. Immediately, there was silence from Aden, and I had to stifle a laugh. Apparently, the chiding from his friend was much more effective than a lecture from Mom.

As adults, we need to make sure we are surrounding ourselves with friends who can do the same for us, friends who will call us out when we are in the wrong and lift us up when we are down. We need friends who can speak truth into our lives even when it is not easy to hear. Think about your peer group today. Are you surrounding yourself with true friends or with those who simply tell you what you want to hear? Get honest with yourself and decide if it's time to make some new friends. Some of the greatest gifts we can have in this life are people who will stand beside us and love us through good and bad. Choose your company wisely. It's vital to your success.

For Deeper Study

> As iron sharpens iron, so one man sharpens another. (Prov. 27:17)

> Two are better than one, because they have a good return for their work: If one falls down, his friend can help him up. But pity the man who falls and has no one to help him up! (Eccles. 4:9–10)

> Do not be misled: "Bad company corrupts good character." (1 Cor. 15:33)

Application Questions

Who in your peer group is an asset to your success? Who in your peer group is detrimental to your development? How can you plan more time with those who are a benefit to you? Do you need to reduce or eliminate the time you are spending with certain friends?

Do It for Me

Young children, and sometimes even us adults, often wish other people would do tasks for us. After all, it would be easier if someone else did my dishes and picked up my house. Aden is no exception to this, and one day, when he was little, I asked him to pick up some papers off the floor and throw them away. He has always been into arts and crafts, and as a result, my house has always been littered with cut-up papers, dangerous loose staples, glue on everything, and don't even get me started on Slime and glitter. But on this particular day, when I asked Aden to clean up the papers, he took a different approach. Without even looking up from what he was doing, he very smugly retorted, "Maybe you will pick them up and throw them away." A lot of sass for a little guy, but oftentimes, we take this approach when God asks something of us.

We might know we need to change something or take a step in the direction God is calling us, but instead, we ask God to do it for us. We ask Him to take the temptation away rather than choosing to stay away from it ourselves. Or we ask Him to force us into doing what we need to do when really, He's calling us to act in faith. The Bible tells us that God has already given us power and authority as well as "everything we need for life and godliness" (2 Pet. 1:3). We have no excuses for not doing what God has called us to. It's time we stopped asking God to "do for us" what He has already given us the ability to do for ourselves. Whatever you are being called to do today, take the step of faith and stop waiting for God to make it easier or take it away. He rewards those who are faithful even when it is difficult.

For Deeper Study

> His divine power has given us everything we need for life and godliness through our knowledge of him who called us by his own glory and goodness. (2 Pet. 1:3)

> I have given you authority to trample on snakes and scorpions and to overcome all the power of the enemy; nothing will harm you. (Luke 10:19)

Application Questions

What is God calling you to take action on right now? How can you take responsibility and start moving forward in this situation?

Know It All

When kids are young, we think it is cute and funny when they think they know it all. When they become teenagers, we often get frustrated by this attitude. But I think God must often look at us like teenagers. We think somehow we know more than God and our answers are better than His. Aden often likes to ask a question and then correct the person when they give him an answer. He was playing this game one day when he was six and he asked me, "What's the smallest thing in the world?"

I responded, "An atom."

Aden began to laugh and responded, "No! You are ridiculous at this game! It's a pebble." Nothing like being berated by a child. Clearly, he knew so much more than me about the world. How could I even think that atoms are smaller than pebbles? And as silly as that is, that's how we often talk to God. We try to correct Him or second-guess the all-knowing God of the universe.

My child was trusting what he could see. To him, a pebble was the smallest object that he could physically see. But my knowledge of science told me that there are things smaller than what we can see with our eyes. In the same way, God is often telling us about things that we cannot see, but we must choose to trust Him. We must learn not to rely on our physical senses as much as on our spiritual knowledge of God and His Word. Today, choose to accept by faith what God is telling you. Do not question or correct Him. After all, He is never wrong. We can take Him at His word.

For Deeper Study

> Then Jesus told him, "Because you have seen me, you have believed; blessed are those who have not seen and yet have believed." (John 20:29)

> Do you still not see or understand? Are your hearts hardened? Do you have eyes but not see, and ears but fail to hear? (Mark 8:17b–18a)

Application Questions

Is there something you need to trust God about today? How can you activate your faith in this area?

Believing

I got a good chuckle one night at bedtime when Aden was three. Bedtime was a constant struggle for us, and we spent hours every night trying to mitigate endless complaints of "I'm hungry. I'm thirsty. I'm hot, cold, scared." And so on and so forth. My usual response to Aden's complaint of being scared was, "Mommy and Seth are right here. The doggies are right here, and God is watching over you, so there's nothing to be scared about. Now go to sleep."

This particular night, though, when I assured Aden that God was protecting him, he shot back a response, "What? Does He have magical powers or something?"

I stifled a laugh, rolled my eyes, and said, "Yup. He does. Now go to bed."

This conversation mirrors the fact that as adults, accepting things by faith often seems difficult. We may have moments where we question if God's promises to us are true. After all, sometimes the things we are believing for take years to come to fulfillment. Abraham had to wait twenty years for his promised child to arrive, but the Bible tells us that his faith is what made him be considered righteous. Whatever God is calling you to believe for, keep holding on to your faith. There are blessings beyond comprehension waiting for you if you hold to your faith, no matter how long it takes to see it come to pass.

For Deeper Study

> Abraham believed the Lord, and He credited it to him as righteousness. (Gen. 15:6)

> Blessed is she who has believed that what the Lord has said to her will be accomplished. (Luke 1:45)

Application Questions

What are you believing God for in your life? Where can you begin to exercise your faith and trust God for more?

When the Spirit Moves You

I must confess to you that I am a person who does not enjoy dancing. I have never had a great rhythm, and although I love watching
expert dancers who can seem to move with perfect ease and timing
to any beat, I am not one of those. As a result of this, I try to avoid
situations in which dancing might become necessary. After all, I don't
want to look silly. Children, however, seem to have not a care in the
world when it comes to dancing. They don't mind looking foolish,
and they aren't concerned with how their dance moves look or even
if anyone is looking. Case in point, Aden and I were out to dinner at
a Chinese restaurant one night. He was eight years old, and we were
having a nice talk. He randomly, during our conversation, dropped
his fork and did something akin to the Dab. Although I'm not sure
it could really be titled as such. I laughed a little and asked, "What
was that?"

His response, "I don't know. It just felt right." I laughed even
harder at this. But you know what, dancing and moving in worship
to our God is a completely biblical concept.

We should never be afraid to "do what feels right" in worship.
Maybe you feel God calling you to lift your hands, kneel on the floor,
or jump up and down during worship. We should never be afraid or
embarrassed to express our love and gratefulness to our God. King
David went as far as to dance openly and jump about in the streets in
front of his subjects. His wife, at the time, was quite appalled that he
would act this way. After all, it was far from dignified. God, however,
saw David's act of worship as beautiful and holy, and nothing that
God deems as good can be labeled not so. This week, as you feel the
Spirit move you to praise God, do not hold back. You never look
foolish to God when you give Him your wholehearted praise.

For Deeper Study

> King David, wearing a linen ephod, danced before the Lord with all his might. (2 Sam. 6:14)

> I will celebrate before the Lord. I will become even more undignified than this. (2 Sam. 6:21b–22a)

Application Questions

Have you been holding back your worship for fear of looking silly? How can you begin to let go of your pride and worship God more fully?

Who's Your Daddy?

From a very young age, Aden has had a knack for embarrassing me in public. In fact, I have shared some of these moments with you already. One particularly embarrassing moment occurred at a restaurant during lunch hour. It was a weekday, and Aden and I were eating lunch surrounded by a large crowd of retired people. We were quietly enjoying our meal when out of nowhere, Aden stood up at the table, looked directly at me, and yelled, "Do you even know who my daddy is?" I was mortified to say the least. I did, in fact, know exactly who his dad was (as did he), and I proceeded to loudly let him know this as there were many concerned glances from the tables around us.

The truth is that whether or not you know who your physical father is, and whether or not you had a good relationship with that person can have a lot of bearing on how you perceive yourself. No matter what relationship you have with your biological father, though, you can be assured of who your heavenly Father is. He has promised to never leave you or forsake you, and you can find your identity in Him. He has called you as an heir to all the goodness He has, and you can take confidence in knowing that you are His child.

For Deeper Study

> I will never leave you nor forsake you. (Josh. 1:5b)

> Because those who are led by the Spirit of God are sons of God. For you did not receive a spirit that makes you a slave again to fear, but you received the Spirit of sonship. And by him we cry, "Abba, Father." The Spirit himself testifies with our spirit that we are God's children. Now if we are children, then we are heirs—heirs of God and co-heirs with Christ, if indeed we share in his sufferings in order that we may also share in his glory. (Rom. 8:14–17)

Application Questions

Do you know who you are in Christ? Do you see God as your Father? How can you begin to live more confidently as a result of the knowledge of who your "dad" is?

Just My Luck

We all have things we dislike doing. Perhaps it is taking out the garbage or washing the dishes. And then there are those experiences that are unpleasant realities of life: waiting at the DMV, getting calls from telemarketers, or being put on hold when you make an important phone call. For an eight year old, some of the worst things in life are the simple things that need taken care of on a yearly basis—dental appointments and doctor visits. One day, I decided to be very productive and scheduled Aden a haircut and a dental appointment on the same day. To my mind, this was a winning day in which I would be killing two birds with one stone. To Aden's thinking, this was the worst day ever. He loudly proclaimed, "First a haircut, then the dentist! What's next? Shots?" Now I had not scheduled any shots into our day, but by his observations, that would be the logical next step.

We as adults often make these hasty assumptions about what might happen next to us. Have you ever heard someone make the statement, "That's just my luck," when something bad happened to them? Or maybe you yourself have a tendency to make negative comments about your future, saying things like, "I'll probably get stuck in traffic. That's just how my life is." Or, "Typical me, always messing something up." If you are prone to making negative declarations over your life, I want to urge you right now to *stop*! The words you speak have incredible power, and you can speak good or evil into your day simply with the things you are declaring. If you are expecting and speaking negative all day, you will most likely receive negative. If you are expecting and speaking positive, the results will tend to be positive. Take some time to listen to what's coming out of your mouth today, and if what you're speaking isn't what you want, it's time to make a change.

For Deeper Study

> The tongue has the power of life and death, and those who love it will eat its fruit. (Prov. 18:21)

> This day I call heaven and earth as witnesses against you that I have set before you life and death, blessings and curses. Now choose life, so that you and your children may live. (Deut. 30:19)

Application Questions

What kinds of things have you been speaking lately? What are some positive things you can start speaking on a daily basis?

Bite Your Tongue

If you have ever dealt with a sassy child, you are well aware of the fact that their comments can be infuriating and hilarious at the same time. One such moment occurred at the grocery store, where so many of Aden's incidents tend to happen. After all, there is nothing like a captive audience in the checkout line to spur on a child's worst behavior. Aden was doing something which elicited a reprimand from me; but in response, rather than a demure, "Yes, ma'am," he quickly yelled out, "You shut your mouth!" I was shocked and embarrassed that my four-year-old would act this way in public, but I wonder how many times it would benefit us if we had someone who told us this more often.

I know personally there are many times when I would have been better off if someone would have advised me to be quiet. Perhaps you can relate? Maybe it was that argument with a loved one where you spouted off some hurtful words you can't take back. You may have let slip some gossip about a coworker or friend that you later regretted having said. We have a tendency to get ourselves in trouble with our mouths, and sometimes we need to tell ourselves to stop talking. The scripture tells us that the tongue wields great power and is like a little spark which can start a raging fire. We would do well to choose our words wisely and not allow our emotions to govern our mouths.

For Deeper Study

> Likewise the tongue is a small part of the body, but it makes great boasts. Consider what a great forest is set on fire by a small spark. The tongue also is a fire, a world of evil among the parts of the body. It corrupts the whole person, sets the whole course of his life on fire, and is itself set on fire by hell. (James 3:5–6)

> When words are many, sin is not absent, but he who holds his tongue is wise. (Prov. 10:19)

Application Questions

Is there an area of your life where you need to start watching your tongue? Perhaps it's with a friend group or a person who frustrates you. How can you remind yourself today to choose your words wisely?

Mayonnaise and Other Condiments

The Word of God can sometimes be a bit confusing, and often-times, the old King James Version can have some tricky sayings that would make any adult scratch their head, let alone a child. As Aden has come up through the years, we have had many a good laugh about his interpretations of the scriptures. Case in point, we were having a conversation after Sunday school one day about the children of Israel and their time in the wilderness. Aden remarked, "Eew, God fed the Israelites manna? That's so gross. That's just mean!"

I was confused by this as I thought it was pretty nice of God to give them free food in the desert for forty years. "Why?" I asked. "Do you know what manna is?"

Aden quickly replied, "Ya, it's a dressing."

When I finally stopped laughing, I let him know that the word he was thinking of was *mayonnaise*, and that was not what the Israelites ate.

Another such incident happened with a verse I often quote: "He will make my feet like hind's feet, and He shall make me to walk upon mine high places" (Hab. 3:19, KJV). I say this verse as a reminder to myself that God is taking me higher and giving me the ability to go to new levels, like the "hind," a type of mountain deer which has incredible climbing ability. Aden, after hearing me say this in the car one day, questioned, "Why do you want your feet to be like ketchup?"

I asked, "What are you talking about?" He calmly explained to me that he had heard me saying this last week and had asked his dad what a Heinz was. His father, of course, not knowing the context, had told him it was a type of ketchup.

It can be easy to get confused about scripture verses, which is why it is so important to have teachers in your life. Invest in a good study Bible and attend church or listen to audios which teach you about the Word of God. There is so much to learn, and we cannot learn it all on our own. It's important to take time to listen and be taught.

For Deeper Study

> Study to show thyself approved unto God, a workman who needeth not to be ashamed, rightly dividing the word of truth. (2 Tim. 2:15, KJV)

> Test everything. Hold onto the good. (1 Thess. 5:21)

(King James Version references were taken from biblegateway.com.)

Application Questions

Are you actively involved with some type of biblical teaching weekly? What steps can you take to increase your learning in the area of biblical knowledge?

Saying the Right Thing

Have you ever tried to say something which you thought at the time was helpful or correct, but in hindsight, you realized it was not the best thing? We can probably all relate to the experience of having "put our foot in our mouth," so to speak. Children often say things too which may not come out exactly as they want them to. At three years old, Aden told me one day as I was painting my fingernails, "Aw, that's so pretty, Mom! You look like a big purple monster." To his credit, in his mind, this was probably a great compliment. To me, it was not so flattering.

The Apostle Peter had some of these not-so-great speaking moments too, moments where he thought he had nailed it with the perfect statement, only to be put in his place by Jesus. Moments like these can be embarrassing, but there are two ways to handle them. One, don't be afraid to own up to making a mistake. Be willing to apologize and move on if you've made an unwise statement. Two, ask the Holy Spirit to give you guidance and look to Him for the words to speak in tricky situations. You will find that God can give you just the words you need when you aren't sure what the best answer is. If you will seek Him first, you can avoid a lot of these "uh-oh" moments in the future.

For Deeper Study

> And Peter took him [Jesus] aside and began to rebuke him. But when Jesus turned and looked at his disciples, he rebuked Peter. "Get behind me, Satan!" he said. "You do not have in mind the things of God, but the things of men." (Mark 8:32b–33)

> As the men were leaving Jesus, Peter said to him, "Master, it is good for us to be here. Let us put up three shelters—one for you, one for Moses, and one for Elijah." (He did not know what he was saying.) (Luke 9:33)

> When you are brought before synagogues, rulers, and authorities, do not worry about how you will defend yourselves or what you will say, for the Holy Spirit will teach you at that time what you should say. (Luke 12:11–12)

> He who guards his lips guards his life, but he who speaks rashly will come to ruin. (Prov. 13:3)

Application Question

Can you think of a time when you spoke before thinking? Begin to be more conscientious of your words this week.

Free Jobs

Have you ever noticed that children seem to have an appreciation for things that adults don't have? They seem to find wonder and joy in everything. It is a rare and refreshing thing to find an adult with that kind of joy and gratitude in life. One such example of this comes in the area of work. I know many of us grumble and complain about our day-to-day jobs. Although they provide us our income, many of us are unhappy with them and would rather not go if given the option. Aden, as a child, however, has not had the opportunity to become disillusioned by the frustrations of a job. So one day, in search of a way to make some money, he asked me, "How old do I have to be to get a job?" I told him that fifteen was usually the age that someone could get a job in our state. He then asked me a more peculiar question. "How much does it cost to get a job?"

"Nothing?" I said, rather confused by his question.

He immediately responded enthusiastically, "You can get a job for free?" His excitement caught me off guard. After all, a job requires me to put my time and effort in, why should I have to pay for it as well? But to a child, this fact was an exciting prospect, an opportunity that could be seized, and he had not lost the ability to appreciate that.

As we age, we must strive to not lose our joy and appreciation for the gifts God has given us. I have heard the expression that someone else is praying to have the exact things you have taken for granted. Maybe you are tired of your small apartment. There is a homeless person that would love to have a living space to call their own. Maybe your job seems mundane and you've lost your excitement for it. There's a man who just got laid off who would take that boring job in a heartbeat. We must never forget that every good thing we have is a blessing from God, and we should learn to appreciate and be thankful for it. Today, find reasons to be thankful and full of joy. Try looking at your circumstances in a new light. You just might be amazed at how many good things you have.

For Deeper Study

> This is the day that the Lord has made; let us rejoice and be glad in it. (Ps. 118:24)

> Worship the Lord with gladness; come before him with joyful songs. (Ps. 100:2)

> Every good and perfect gift is from above, coming down from the Father of the heavenly lights, who does not change like shifting shadows. (James 1:17)

Application Question

What have you been taking for granted in your life? Make a list of things you can express thankfulness for today.

The Truth Hurts

Have you ever heard the expression, "I'm just being honest." Usually, that is said right after someone has said something hurtful, and it is used to excuse or justify them saying the hurtful thing. The Bible, while encouraging us to speak the truth, adds an important instruction. Speak the truth *in love*. This means that when we are thinking about saying something that may be potentially hurtful to someone, we need to evaluate if we are saying it out of love or simply to make ourselves look better. Aden, as a small child, had a habit of complaining about whatever I made for dinner, no matter what food I made. One night, knowing that he would probably get in trouble for making a rude comment, he tried to supplement his statement with something positive. After glancing at his plate, he remarked, "Wow! This looks really gross, but I'm sure since you made it, it will taste good. But it looks really gross."

In the case of Aden and the dinner plate, what he said didn't need to be stated at all; and similarly, we could many times stop ourselves from making rude comments that would be better off left unsaid if we would apply the "speaking the truth in love" rule. Maybe you need to tell a friend that their actions were hurtful to you, but you don't need to also point out everything else you think they need to work on when doing so. Or perhaps your spouse didn't do a task the way you asked them to. It may be true that the bedspread is on sideways, but if the bed is made, it's not necessary or loving to criticize his or her efforts. We could avoid hurting a lot of people if we will simply learn to temper our words with love. Begin evaluating the things you say today and see what you can state in a more loving way, or perhaps not state at all.

For Deeper Study

> Instead, speaking the truth in love, we will in all things grow up into him who is the Head, that is Christ. From him, the whole body, joined and held together by every supporting ligament, grows and builds itself up in love, as each part does its work. (Eph. 4:15)

> Be kind and compassionate to one another, forgiving each other just as in Christ God forgave you. (Eph. 4:32)

> Do not let any unwholesome talk come out of your mouths, but only what is helpful for building others up according to their needs, that it may benefit those who listen. (Eph. 4:29)

Application Questions

Who have you hurt with your words lately? Do you need to start working on adding love to your speech and interactions with others? How can you do that today?

Jackpot

If you are anything like me, you've probably wished at some point or another in your life that you could just win the lottery, and then all your problems in life would be solved. After all, if we just had more money, more time, more—you name it—then life would be good. Success, however, does not work like that. It is not an overnight happening. It requires persistent, day in and day out work. Savings must be acquired one dollar at a time, and debt paid off in the same way. Sometimes, though, our goals and dreams can seem so far away that we want to just lay down and take a nap. We think our efforts aren't getting us anywhere so we should just go to sleep.

I was having a day like this, once, and I declared, "I'm just going to go lie down, buddy."

Without so much as missing a beat, Aden sternly replied, "You have to start acting like a full-adult grown-up, Mom. You can't just lie down and sleep. You need to work."

Those words were not very appreciated in the moment, but they held a lot of truth. If we want to be mature and achieve any measure of success and peace in our lives, we must learn to work. Now I am not suggesting that you overwork yourself, and I believe there is a valuable place for rest in our lives too. But I think we all can admit there are areas in our lives where we have been avoiding doing the work, and it's time for us to step out and get it done. Maybe you have been sleeping in instead of hitting the gym like you know you should. Maybe you tell yourself it's been a long day, you'll just go to bed early tonight and tomorrow you will read that book. Whatever it is that you know you need to do, whatever steps you need to take, it's time to stop sleeping and get to work. Roll up your sleeves and put in the effort this week. Over time, your work will pay off, and that is worth all the extra effort.

For Deeper Study

> A little sleep, a little slumber, a little folding of the hands to rest—and poverty will come on you like a bandit and scarcity like an armed man. (Prov. 24:33–34)

> The plans of the diligent lead to profit as surely as haste leads to poverty. (Prov. 21:5)

Application Questions

Have you been avoiding something you know you need to do? What habits or routines can you begin this week that will take you closer to your goals?

Being Sneaky

Kids can be very sly when they are trying to get something their way. Oftentimes, we catch on to what they are up to before too long, but it can be amusing to see the ways they try to bamboozle us. Aden has always been the great excuse inventor when it comes to bedtime. One night, though, he tried a slightly different approach. I was watching a show and enjoying a bag of popcorn when he came wandering out of his room. "Mom," he said. "Sometimes I have this weird feeling that I'm only like half of me, like I'm not even a person." Slowly, he edged over, took a handful of popcorn, and sat down next to me. Then he asked, "Can I watch TV with you?" Ah, the real motive came out!

Rolling my eyes, I reassured him, "Aden, you are a real person. Now get your hands out of my popcorn and go back to bed."

Oftentimes, we try to give ourselves little false motives for why we are doing things too. You just have to share that piece of gossip about your coworker, but you tell yourself it's because you're "concerned" about that person. You snap at your spouse because they annoyed you, but really, it's because you're wrestling with guilt over not being a perfect parent. God isn't fooled by the false reasoning we use on ourselves. He sees right through to what we're really up to. It's time to get honest with ourselves and own up to our actions. This week, stop and think before you do something, and make sure you really do have pure motives. After all, the only ones we fool with false pretenses are ourselves.

For Deeper Study

> The purposes of a man's heart are deep waters,
> but a man of understanding draws them out.
> (Prov. 20:5)

> All a man's ways seem right to him, but the Lord
> weighs the heart. (Prov. 21:2)

Application Questions

Have you been operating under false pretenses in an area of your life? How can you hold yourself accountable for your actions and motives this week?

Prayer Time

Kids say the best prayers. They don't have pretense or worry about saying the right thing. They just say what's on their minds, and honestly, I think that's how it was intended to be. Jesus was not impressed by the Pharisee's articulate and rehearsed prayers. He encouraged us to pray for our daily needs, to ask for help, to glorify God, and to seek forgiveness. He also modeled for us the idea of praying often and in all things. Prayer is simply talking to God, but even that idea can be somewhat intimidating. He is God after all.

Whenever Aden and I do our devotions together, I always ask him if he would like me to pray, or if he would like to say the prayer. One night, he decided he would like to do the praying. We bowed our heads and closed our eyes, and this is what he prayed. "Dear God, please help my mom work on her stress. Amen." Personally, I thought I had been doing quite well managing my stress that day, but apparently, Aden thought it could use some intervention from a higher power.

We as adults should learn to pray this way all the time, with everything we are doing. We should get in the habit of constantly thanking God, asking for help, praising Him, and lifting up others as we go about our day. The more we communicate with God, the stronger our relationship will be. Trust me, that is a great way to work on your stress.

For Deeper Study

And when you pray, do not be like the hypocrites, for they love to pray standing in the synagogues and on the street corners to be seen by men. I tell you the truth, they have received their reward in full. But when you pray, go into your room, close the door and pray to your Father, who is unseen. Then your Father, who sees what is done in secret, will reward you. And when you pray, do not keep on babbling like pagans, for they think they will be heard because of their many words. Do not be like them, for your Father knows what you need before you ask him. This, then, is how you should pray: "Our Father in heaven, hallowed be your name, your kingdom come, your will be done on earth as it is in heaven. Give us today our daily bread. Forgive us our debts, as we have also forgiven our debtors. And lead us not into temptation, but deliver us from the evil one." (Matt. 6:5–13)

Pray continually. (1 Thess. 5:17)

Application Questions

How can you increase your prayer life and begin to pray more frequently and genuinely? Is there an area you have been avoiding talking to God about? Take it to Him in conversation today.

Figuring It Out

Children seem to have a sureness about themselves and who they are that adults seem to have lost somewhere in the process of growing up. If you ask a child who they are and what they are going to do, they almost always have an immediate and definite answer. "I am Aden, and I am a ninja," was a very common response at our house. As adults sometimes, though, we question our identity and self-worth. We question if we are good enough, talented enough, or capable enough to do what we feel we should. One day, when Aden and I were watching a movie together, the main character remarked, "I just have no idea who I am." Aden looked at me very seriously and said, "That was like totally me...when I was three."

So self-assured, so at home with who they are, children can teach us something about learning to live with ourselves. Growing into our best selves is a constant and ever-changing process. We have to get comfortable with who we are and where we are going. The Bible tells us that God is continually making us better and better. It's okay to accept that you aren't perfect yet. None of us ever will be on this earth. But are you better off than you were a few years ago? If so, you know that you are moving in the right direction. And if not, it's not too late to start. God has a great plan for each and every one of us, and it starts with you, just who you are.

For Deeper Study

> And we, who with unveiled faces all reflect the Lord's glory, are being transformed into his likeness with ever-increasing glory, which comes from the Lord, who is the Spirit. (2 Cor. 3:18)

> The path of the righteous is like the first gleam of dawn, shining ever brighter till the full light of day. (Prov. 4:18)

Application Questions

Have you been struggling with your identity in Christ? What are some areas you have made improvements in over the last several months or years? What are some areas you can begin to grow in, and what steps can you take to start moving in the right direction?

Breaking the Rules

Children have a knack for picking up on all our bad habits as parents, as much as we try to hide them. Aden asked me one day in the car, "Mom, do you text and drive?"

"Sometimes," I replied.

"Mom!" He yelled. "The radio says you're not supposed to do that!" Nothing like being put in place by a six-year-old.

Our spiritual lives can be a lot like this also. We know we shouldn't do something, but we still do it anyway, thinking we can get away with it. It's just a little thing, right?

The Apostle Paul tells us that even he struggled with doing things he knew weren't right. The good news is that once we believe in Christ, He is no longer judging us or condemning us for our actions. We can know that we are covered by grace, and God does not cast us out for our mistakes but loves us as we continue to grow and get better. It is the knowledge of this grace that should compel us to move away from our sins and toward God's holiness. Fear of condemnation is a motivator for some, but gratitude for grace is a much more powerful and beautiful incentive to do and become better. Whatever wrongdoing you are wrestling with today, know that you are set free from it, and that God has given you the power and the freedom to do what's right.

For Deeper Study

> I do not understand what I do. For what I want to do I do not do, but what I hate I do. And if I do what I do not want to do, I agree that the law is good. As it is, it is no longer I myself who do it, but it is sin living in me. I know that nothing good lives in me, that is, in my sinful nature. For I have the desire to do what is good, but I cannot carry it out. For what I do is not the good I want to do; no, the evil I do not want to do—this I keep on doing. (Rom. 7:15–19)

> Therefore, there is now no condemnation for those who are in Christ Jesus, because through Christ Jesus the law of the Spirit of life set me free from the law of sin and death. (Rom. 8:1–2)

Application Questions

What sins have you been wrestling with in your life? Does knowing that you are not condemned help you to let go of guilt and move forward into doing what is right?

Unanswered Questions

I am not sure why it is that children are so inquisitive, but they can sure drive adults crazy with some of the things they ask. For example, Aden asked me one day, "A peregrine falcon can dive at 205 miles per hour, so how many millimeters is that per second?" Now theoretically, I could do the math and the conversions and come up with an answer. Not while I'm driving though. What possible use could a child have for this information?

We tend to forget though, that our questions to God come across a lot like this. Oftentimes, it's not that God can't answer the questions we throw at Him; but that most of the time, we don't need to know the answers. We just need to know that God is in control, and if we trust Him, that is answer enough. Frustrating? Yes. Discouraging? At times. But it is in our unanswered questions that we can begin to exercise true faith. After all, faith is believing even when we don't see; and if God answered all our questions, we wouldn't need faith. So next time life hits you with a challenging question, and you're tempted to get angry at God for not answering, remember that God is greatly pleased by your faith, and that trusting Him without having all the answers is exactly what we were meant to do.

For Deeper Study

> And without faith it is impossible to please God, because anyone who comes to him must believe that He exists and that He rewards those who earnestly seek him. (Heb. 11:6)

> Then Job replied to the Lord: "I know that you can do all things; no plan of yours can be thwarted. You asked, 'Who is this that obscures my counsel without knowledge?' Surely I spoke of things I did not understand, things too wonderful for me to know. You said, 'Listen now, and I will speak. I will question you, and you shall answer me.' My ears had heard of you but now my eyes have seen you." (Job 42:1–5)

Application Questions

What questions have you been asking of God lately? How can you exercise your faith in relationship to these questions?

Self-Inflicted Injuries

Have you ever had a bad habit that you knew was harmful to you and your life, but you kept doing it anyway? Maybe you drink too much pop even though you know it's not good for your teeth or waistline. Perhaps you stay up too late and then have trouble getting up on time in the morning. We all have negative things we wrestle with, and a lot of them are a result of our own actions.

One day, at the age of seven, Aden came out of his room and asked me to make him a dental appointment. "Why?" I asked him.

"Because my mouth hurts when I bite my tongue," he replied simply.

Now to an adult, the answer was obvious. You don't need a professional to fix your problem. You just need to stop biting your tongue. How similar though that many of us go to God continually in prayer, asking for more money, but we refuse to stop frivolous spending; seeking help to get our health on track, but not following the doctor's orders; and on and on the list goes. Now I am not denying that we need the power of God in our lives to help us overcome our bad habits, but I am suggesting that in addition to petitioning God for help, we pick ourselves up and begin taking action to end our negative behaviors. God gave us free will and the ability to control our own actions, and we are free to choose what we will do. He will not force us into doing the right thing. God has given us self-control, and it is time we exercise it. We need to stop simply asking someone else to help us, and step out and do what we know we should.

For Deeper Study

> For God did not give us a spirit of timidity, but of power, of love, and of self-discipline. (2 Tim. 1:7)

> This day I call heaven and earth as witnesses against you that I have set before you life and death, blessings and curses. Now choose life, so that you and your children may live. (Deut. 30:19)

> If you do what is right, will you not be accepted? But if you do not do what is right, sin is crouching at your door; it desires to have you, but you must master it. (Gen. 4:7)

Application Questions

What negative habits have you been harboring in your life? What actions or steps can you take this week to eradicate destructive behavior?

Be Like Me

I have to admit that I am going to break from the pattern of Adenisms with this story. The tale I am going to share here is not about Aden. I was eating lunch at McDonald's one day when a little girl came in with what appeared to be her grandmother. There was a woman there who knew the grandmother, and she introduced herself to the little girl. "Hi, what's your name?" She politely asked.

"Olivia," stated the little girl matter-of-factly.

"That's a pretty name," remarked the woman.

Smiling smugly, the little girl looked up and said, "Now do you wish your name was Olivia?"

Oh, to have the confidence of a small child. But in fact, this is the way Jesus wants us to be with the world. We should live in such a way that people are attracted to our faith.

Are you an attractive Christian? Do you go around with confidence and joy? Or are you going around dejected, with a negative attitude, grumbling and complaining? As Christians, we are called to be the lights of the world. We should draw people to ourselves and to our God by the lives we lead. Perhaps you have forgotten that you are on display to a world looking for a solution. Begin today to evaluate your attitude and actions in the light of those who are watching. Is your life something others would want to emulate? If not, go back to the Word of God and begin modeling yourself after Jesus. People followed Him all over the countryside, trying to figure out what it was that caused Him to be so radically different. If you live by His example, you cannot fail to attract people to the Father.

For Deeper Study

You are the light of the world. A city on a hill cannot be hidden. Neither do people light a lamp and put it under a bowl. Instead they put it on its stand, and it gives light to everyone in the house. In the same way, let your light shine before men, that they may see your good deeds and praise your Father in heaven. (Matt. 5:14–16)

He said to them, "Go into all the world and preach the good news to all creation." (Mark 16:15)

By their fruit you will recognize them.... Likewise every good tree bears good fruit, but a bad tree bears bad fruit. (Matt. 7:16a–17)

Application Questions

What type of "fruit" are you displaying to those around you? Are you being a light in your everyday life? What about your life is pointing others to Christ? How can you begin to live a life that will cause others to seek God?

Empty Threats

Have you ever felt threatened before? It can be quite scary thinking there is someone who has got it out for you. You feel as if you must watch your back at every turn. Sometimes, however, we can tell when a threat is not to be taken seriously. For example, Aden once told me, "If you don't be nice to me, Seth is going to put bread on your head and throw you in the toilet!" I knew right away that my husband would do no such thing, so I had nothing to fear.

Oftentimes though, we allow ourselves to live in fear of the threats the devil throws at us. They are lies and manipulations, but for some reason, we talk ourselves into believing them. We forget that we have the power within us to negate the threats Satan levels against us. If you are feeling fearful today, I encourage you to remember that fear is a lie from the pit of hell. Fear is not of God; in fact, God says that His perfect love will cast out all fear. Begin to stand up to the lies today and shake off the threats that cause you to feel inferior. You are a child of the Most High God, and nothing can threaten your position with Him.

For Deeper Study

> Be self-controlled and alert. Your enemy the devil prowls around like a roaring lion looking for someone to devour. Resist him, standing firm in the faith, because you know that your brothers throughout the world are undergoing the same kind of sufferings. (1 Pet. 5:8–9)

> You, dear children, are from God and have overcome them, because the one who is in you is greater than the one who is in the world. (1 John 4:4)

> For I am convinced that neither death nor life, neither angels nor demons, neither the present nor the future, nor any powers, neither height nor depth, nor anything else in all creation, will be able to separate us from the love of God that is in Christ Jesus our Lord. (Rom. 8:38–39)

> I have told you these things, so that in me you may have peace. In this world you will have trouble. But take heart! I have overcome the world. (John 16:33)

Application Questions

What lies of the enemy have you been believing lately? What truths can you meditate on and speak to defeat the devil's threats?

Say "Thank You"

There are few things more agitating to me than an ungrateful person, particularly when that person is my child. We have always tried to bless Aden with wonderful things, and unfortunately, he has gotten a bit unappreciative at times. Case in point, one year, Aden's dad and stepmom, along with my husband and I, spent quite a bit of money to buy him and two friends tickets to an amusement park for Aden's birthday. Later on that same day, I bought a small candy bar at the grocery store, probably about the equivalent of 95 cents. Aden quickly inquired if he could have some, to which I replied, "No. I bought this for me and Seth."

Rolling his eyes and stomping off in a huff, Aden declared, "I don't know why you have to be so selfish!"

If only he understood how much more we had given him in his tickets to the park, perhaps he would have been more grateful.

Have you ever been like this with God? You didn't get the thing you asked for right now, so you chose to be angry rather than be filled with praise and thankfulness for all the amazing blessings He has already given you. Our salvation alone should be enough to cause us to glorify Him every day, not to mention breath in our lungs, food to eat, homes to live in, safety, jobs, family, health, and on and on the list goes. We can never run out of things to be thankful to God for. Today, choose to be filled with gratitude rather than with the demanding attitude of an entitled child. You are God's child, and He will give you good things in the right time. Start by appreciating what you have, and you might just find that God rewards those who live with a grateful heart.

For Deeper Study

> Every good and perfect gift is from above, coming down from the Father of the Heavenly lights, who does not change like shifting shadows. (James 1:17)

> If you, then, though you are evil, know how to give good gifts to your children, how much more will your Father in heaven give good gifts to those who ask Him. (Matt. 7:11)

> Give thanks in all circumstances, for this is God's will for you in Christ Jesus. (1 Thess. 5:18)

Application Question

What things have you been being ungrateful for in your life? Try writing down and thanking God for at least three things each day this week.

Walking

In order for you to understand the story I am about to tell you, I need you to know that a few years ago, I made the mistake of trying to lug a very heavy box, with the pieces of a dresser in it, by myself. My plan was to get the dresser assembled before my husband got home from work. As it turned out, the box ripped while I was dragging it, and the entire dresser fell out onto my foot, and my husband had to come home early to take me to the emergency room. For the next few days, I had Aden help me out extra by doing things around the house and bringing me things I needed so I didn't have to hobble to get them. He decided to begrudgingly remind me of this a few weeks ago. "Remember when you hurt your foot and I had to do everything for you because you couldn't walk?" He said condescendingly.

"Yes, because there wasn't a whole year before you learned to walk that I had to do everything for you." I quipped back.

This conversation reminded me of the people Jesus encountered during his days on earth who were not able to walk. He was met by several people who were invalids, and each time, He did something interesting. Jesus healed the people who could not walk, but He also gave them a command—to walk. You see, God has promised us that He will help us in the midst of our trials, but He also expects us to do our part. We must get up and walk in faith. We cannot just sit around and wait for everything to be done for us. True healing occurs when we accept God's healing and then begin to move forward in the right direction. Refuse to remain crippled and stuck today. Know that God will help you, but He is calling you to step out.

For Deeper Study

> When Jesus saw him lying there and learned that he had been in this condition for a long time, he asked him, "Do you want to get well?" "Sir," the invalid replied, "I have no one to help me into the pool when the water is stirred. While I am trying to get in, someone else goes down ahead of me." Then Jesus said to him, "Get up! Pick up your mat and walk." At once the man was cured; he picked up his mat and walked. (John 5:6–9a)

> By faith Abraham, when called to go to a place he would later receive as his inheritance, obeyed and went, even though he did not know where he was going. (Heb. 11:8)

> "Lord, if it's you," Peter replied, "tell me to come to you on the water." "Come," he said. Then Peter got down out of the boat, walked on the water and came toward Jesus. (Matt. 14:28–29)

Application Questions

Is there an area of your life you have been waiting for God's restoration in? What step of faith can you take this week?

Tree Climbing

Here are Aden's instructions for climbing a tree: "First, throw your 'graveling' hook up high in the air onto a branch. Give it a little tug. If the branch breaks, don't use that branch. Also, you will need spiky shoes. You should probably wear high heels."

Step-by-step instructions are helpful. They give us specific guidelines and ensure that we know what to do in each situation. Thankfully for us, God left us an instruction manual in His Word. We never have to be at a loss for what to do because He has promised to give us wisdom if we will ask Him, and He has given us so many examples of how to live out our lives here on earth. As you proceed through the days and years ahead, know that you may have to test a few branches. Your first attempt may not always succeed, and that's okay. God gives us the grace to try again. Also know that some situations may be a bit mucky. You may have to put on your spiky shoes and trudge on through. No matter what you encounter in this life though, know that you have a Guide who can walk you through it and a map which will show you the path to take. God has given you all the tools you need. Safe climbing, my friend!

For Deeper Study

> Your word is a lamp to my feet and a light for my path. (Ps. 119:105)

> If any of you lacks wisdom, he should ask God, who gives generously to all without finding fault, and it will be given to him. (James 1:5)

> But when he, the Spirit of truth, comes, he will guide you into all truth. (John 16:13a)

Application Question

What insights have you gained through reading God's Word that you can apply to a situation you are facing right now?

References

Mom's Devotional Bible—New International Version. Zondervan Publication, 1983.

About the Author

K. L. White-Hartman is a wife, mom, and dog lover. She lives in western Pennsylvania with her husband, son, three dogs, and an albino frog. K. L. has experience working in fields ranging from teaching, to finance, food service, and management. She is also the author and designer of the blog: What K. W.'s Thinking (www.whatkwsthinking.blogspot.com).

Some of K. L.'s favorite pastimes are reading, learning, and getting to know others. She also loves enjoying new experiences around the country and the world while traveling with family and friends.

K. L. is passionate about her love for God, and her desire is to convey God's love with others through her writing. She is looking forward to sharing many more stories with her readers.

To stay in touch with K. L. and get the latest on what she's up to, look her up on social media @KLWhiteHartman.

CPSIA information can be obtained
at www.ICGtesting.com
Printed in the USA
BVHW031010140920
588550BV00036B/66